SCHIRMER'S LIBRARY
OF MUSICAL CLASSICS

Vol. 1850

HEINRICH ERNST KAYSER

Op. 20

36 Elementary and Progressive Studies

For the Viola

Transcribed for Viola and edited by

LEONARD MOGILL

ISBN 978-0-7935-5878-0

G. SCHIRMER, Inc.

DISTRIBUTED BY

HAL•LEONARD®
CORPORATION

7777 W. BLUEMOUND RD. P.O. BOX 13819 MILWAUKEE, WI 53213

36 Studies

Transcribed for Viola and edited by
LEONARD MOGILL

HEINRICH ERNST KAYSER, Op. 20

Allegro moderato *Keep the fingers down as often and as long as possible.*

1.

Andante quasi adagio

2.

Allegro

4.

Allegro vivace

5.

Allegro molto

6.

Allegro assai

9.

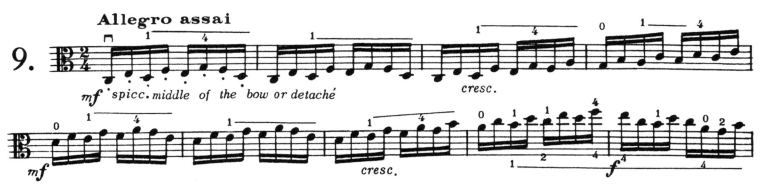

mf *spicc. middle of the bow or detaché*   *cresc.*

Allegro moderato

10.

Allegro energico

11.

mf
Long spicc., middle of the bow

Allegro ma non troppo

12.

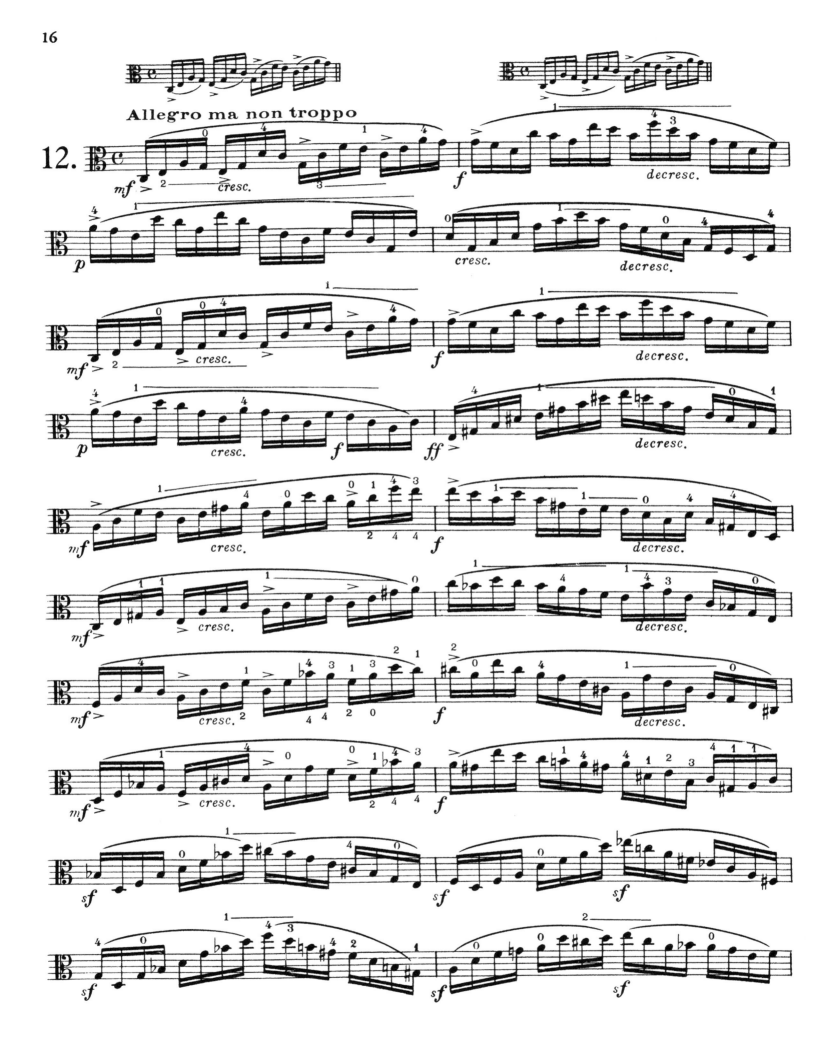

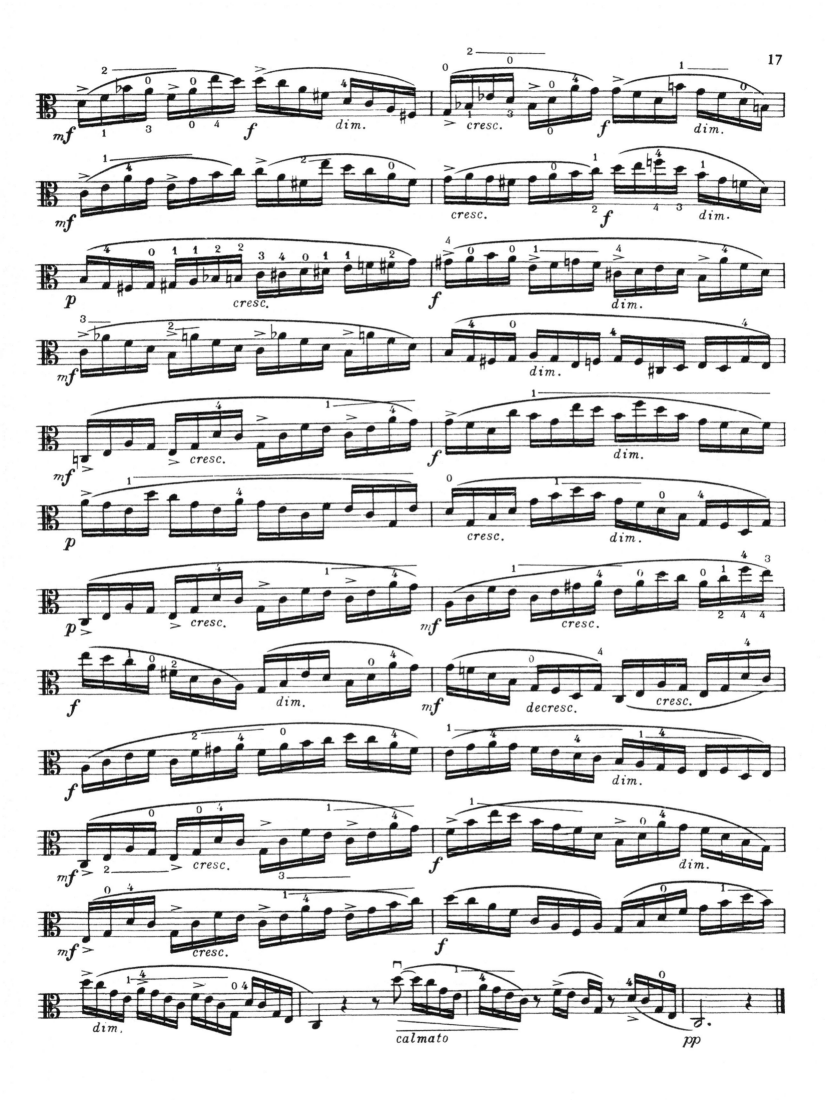

Allegro moderato

15.

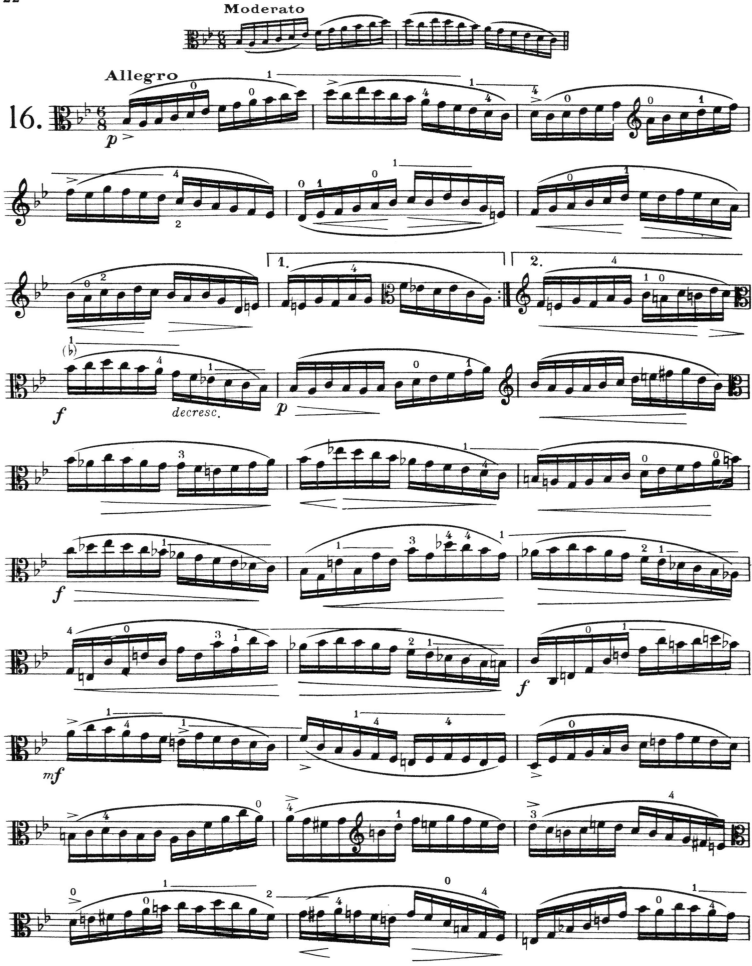

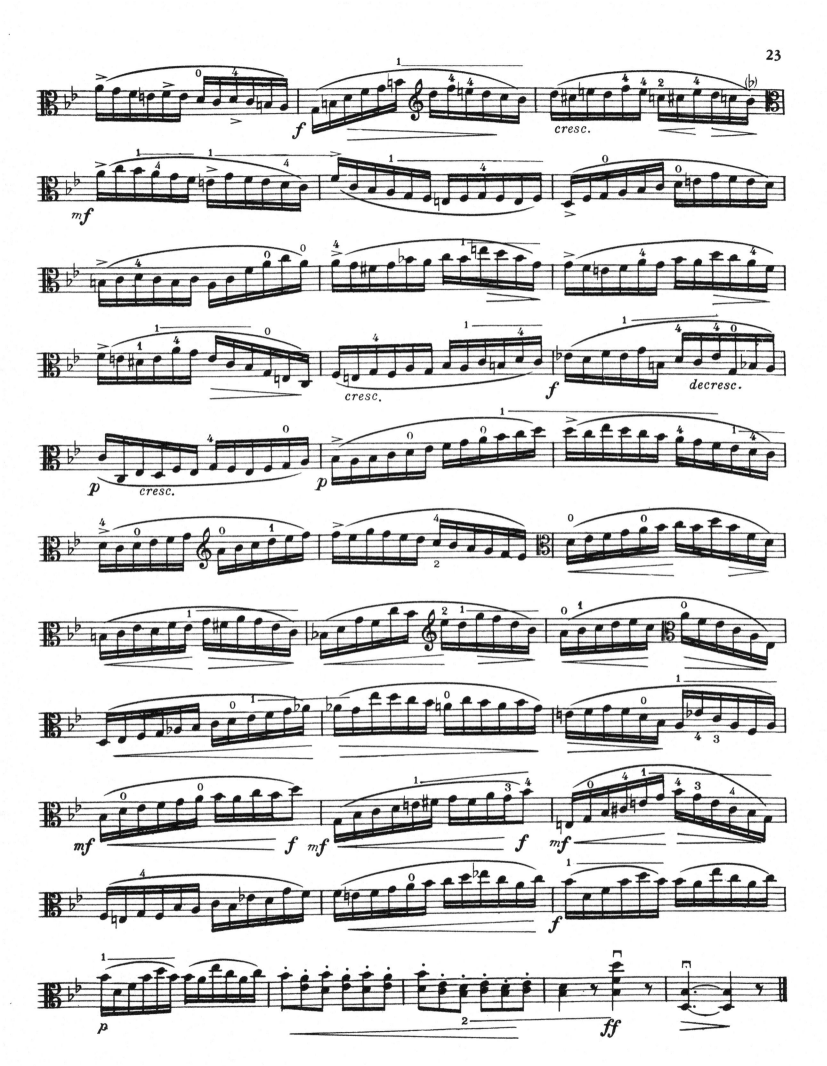

Andante quasi allegretto

17.

Allegro

19.

Allegretto
(near the frog)

20.

Allegro

21.

Allegro assai

22.

Allegretto

at the point

23.

Allegro assai

24.

Allegro

25.

Allegro

27.

28. Allegro assai

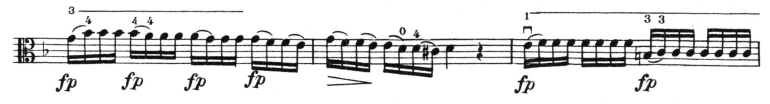

Moderato

29.

Allegro moderato

30.

Allegro molto agitato

31.

44

Allegro moderato

32.

Allegro moderato

Andante poco allegretto

34.

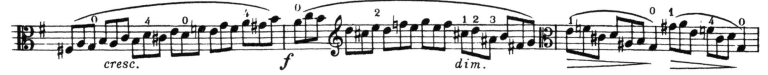

Allegro con fuoco

35.

Allegro
C and G strings.

36.